Journey into Being

By Chris Dewey

Journey into Being

Copyright © Christopher Dewey
All rights reserved.

Printed in the United States of America. No part of this book may be used or reproduced in any manner whatsoever without written permission except in the case of brief quotations embodied in critical articles and reviews.

First time or interested authors, contact Fifth Estate Publishers,
Post Office Box 116, Blountsville, AL 35031.

First Printing June 2007

Cover Design by Matt Owens

Printed on acid-free paper

Library of Congress Control No: 2007929292

ISBN: 1-933580-37-2

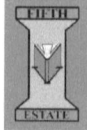

Fifth Estate 2007

The Poems

                                             page

2004   8

    Arrogance of Life
    Delusions
    Empty Room
    Learning Patience
    Nobility
    Sad Old Age
    Words
    Wreckage

2005   24

    A wake or awake
    A-musing
    Beth
    Clouds
    Creating Self
    Dawn
    Dreams I
    Dreams II
    Graham
    Isolation
    Laughter
    Long Hard Night
    Mountaintops
    Nagging Doubts
    Pain
    Smile
    Smooth Stone
    Stranger to Self
    Struggle

                                                                                page

        Train Ride
        Unwanted Child
        Unwanted Offering
        Waiting for Spring

2006   70

        Beginning
        Darkness
        Lesson of the Toys
        Plum Tree
        Prayer
        Sometimes
        Vignettes

2007   84

        Ashes
        Chasm
        Loss
        Muse

Dedication

AJM, BCP, CGN, DBC, EBW, ELP, GDD, JCD, JRD and MAS with thanks for all that I have learned from each of you, for your constant support, your friendship and your love.

Prologue

After I completed the first book of poetry and it actually sold more than one copy, I began to consider the possibility of completing a second volume and putting the photographs in color. The pictures say as much as the words, and perhaps, more. Together, the words and the images form part of the mosaic of my journey.

I'm not sure whether you would call what I write poetic, but it comes from the soul and is an integral part of the discovery process. My poems are at times somber, difficult things, but always there is an undercurrent of hope and trust. The answers will come…in time.

Writing has always held a therapeutic value to me. My words are sign posts on the road of life and are part of my search for life's meaning. To me life is about asking increasingly more elegant questions of the universe in search of its deepest, greatest, most noble truths. Sometimes the questions take the form of scientific enquiry, sometimes they are the mantra for meditative practice, sometimes they take the form of poetry, sometimes they take the form of pictures but always they are being asked by a pilgrim, searching.

Journey into Being

A Collection of Poems

2004 to 2007

The Arrogance of Life

We none of us know death
We only know of death
Through vicarious experience

And we all shall meet death
Exactly as we have lived …

As complete and total amateurs.

As inevitable as my next breath
And ultimately
My last breath …
Death is the great equalizer
It plays no favorites
And knows no partiality

It is merely a question of how we meet
That which can neither be avoided nor denied.

11/04

Delusions

Echoes of words,
Reverberate around me.
I hear them,
But I am not their source.

Visions of living,
Swirl around me.
I see them,
But I am not their source.

How is it that I see not - -
The delusions before me?
How is it that I am so blind?
What is it that shrouds my soul,
With mysteries I cannot penetrate?

Surely this is not the intent.
But if it is not, then when - -
When do the clouds part?
And illusions of what I think is real
Burn away in the light of truth?

12/04

The Empty Room

Alone in my empty room
That some would call a life

I look out
Though murky windows
At a different world
Invisible to others

I cannot describe what I see
Nor even what I feel
For they have no meaning
Outside of this room

And here
Amid the pieces of my world
I see that what we call real
Is only what we choose
Within the confines of each moment.

There seems to be no reason
And yet we cling
With tenacity of purpose

Never once considering the possibility
That what we hold most sacred
Is little more than illusion

11/04

Learning Patience

I wish I could say that I know love.
I wish that the loves that I have known,
Had endured.

But I cannot.

I have always been alone on this Earth;
Never quite being part of the seething throng.

It is as though the world
Happens around me.
And I act as witness,
And sometimes as scribe,
To what I see.

I do not feel this as loss
For it is as it is.
And I have known no other,
That I recall.

This single life,
This momentary illusion,
This transient assembly of atoms;
Is a fabrication for the soul…
Seeking its truest self.

And this is not it,
Nor is it, not it --
Either.

This life is another lesson
Of a patient universe.

09/04

Nobility

There are some;
A very few --
Who understand the price of love.

There are some,
Who commit themselves,
To the uncompromising,
Dedication of self,
And all it might achieve;

To nurture all that is.
And from that synergetic union of purpose,
Emerges all that is most noble about being.

And as they go about their lives,
Without pretension;
These anonymous souls,
Become more than they could have dreamed,
And the universe is a more enlightened place for their passing.

09/04

Sad old age

I look behind her eyes and see the years
Piled up like great rocks
As if each were too heavy to lift

And yet upon her shoulders
She heaved them
And carried them from year to year

So that at life's end --
A heart full of regret and sadness

Has never truly known
The deep freedom of happiness
Or the abiding happiness of freedom

Hers is a life of empty dreams.
And broken hopes.

12/04

Words

Words and actions
Cut and rip
And tear great wounds
In our hearts.

We paper over the cracks
And fill them in with laughter
As if to deny the pain;

As though by covering over
Such gaping wounds
We can re-establish
A semblance of emotional balance.

But the damage done
Is not
So easily hid.

Vulnerable, gasping and lost
We hope for teardrops…
Or a hint of understanding,
To soothe the anguish,

While the world passes by --
Pretending not to see.

11/04

Wreckage

In the battlefield of the soul
Are the memories of the lost,
The dreams of Elysium
And the carnage of the mutilated self.

I often wonder why --

Why do we not submit,
To the baser self?
And abandon the path,
That costs too much to walk.

And yet I will not turn aside,
Or look away.

I struggle with myself
And hope to see a reason,
And use my struggles
As tools of insight.

For we all know conflict

And so it is,
As it is –
Exactly
As we have made it.

12/04

A wake or awake?

We draw our being
From the past
As though it were our reality.

We look at the wake
Of where we have been,
And what we have done,
And we watch the ripples,
Fade into the mists of unknowing.

For nearly fifty years,
I have done no different.

And as I look ahead,
I wonder why.

Have I been so blind for so long?

Does anything I have done in my past,
Define who I might become?

Can anything I know,
Be defined as truth?

Is the wake then, nothing more
Than the brush strokes of ego
Leaving the illusion of a mark?

05/05

A-musing

In an earlier time,
An indifferent smile
Betrayed an empty heart.
A diffident touch,
Was a gesture without meaning.

Such was the parting of the way.

And so she left…
Without a word.

And pathetic-like,
He stood there,
Cutting himself to ribbons,
With self-pity,
And the doubt of what to do…
Without his muse.

But that was then,
And as I said…
An earlier time…

And a different iteration
Of the myriad possibilities.

07/05

Beth

Standing in the doorway,
Ragged clothes, bare feet
Tears in her heart,
But not in her eyes.

The wind on the cliffs
Is more of a friend
Than the bed in her room.

Alone in the world,
She looks outward
To the cold, dark sea

And no-one notices
That, crushed and broken
At her feet
Are the dreams of a little girl.

04/05

Clouds

I thought I knew the sun,
But until the clouds lifted
I had no idea.

I thought I knew myself,
But until the demon left
I had no idea.

I thought I knew the demon,
But until he told me his name
I had no idea.

And for the first time,
In a life's time;

The tears that washed my soul,
Were not just empty droplets,
And not simply for sorrow's sake;

But for something new,
And something wholly - -

…Unexpected.

01/05

Creating Self

Given full rein,
The demons we create,
Could consume and destroy,
All they touch…
Our lives, our loves,
Our hopes and dreams,
Our futures.

It is only through the discipline
Of belief in a higher self,
That we overcome
Our own creations.

And perhaps this is the lesson…
That the demons
Are there
To teach us about ourselves,
To cause us to strive
For a higher purpose…
A more noble self.

So in the fullness of time --
We might see ourselves…
To have lived with honor
Despite ourselves;
And despite the dark abyss,
Into which so many times,
We could so easily,
Have toppled headlong,
Without regret,
Until too late.

For the journey up the mountain,
Is not without peril, snares and chasms.
And if it were --
Would the summit have any value?

04/05

Dawn

We search for meaning,
In the morning of our lives.
We search for connection,
For belonging, and identity.

Too often we find our dearest friend…
Our ego,
And look no further.

It is a sad thing,
To see a man;
And see not his potential.

It is a sad thing to limit self,
To the wiles of ego driven lusts.

In the morning,
As I awoke,
I turned to feel the sun;
And embraced for once…
With all my soul,
The energy of being.

And creeping into dawn,
I almost missed the lesson;

As I have done,
So many times before.

05/05

Dreams

I sift through the rubble of my life.
Kicking over the broken fragments of my dreams.
It is as though some giant cataclysm
Tore through my mind
Leaving devastation in its wake

And in another sense
These are not my dreams alone
They are the splinters and shards
Of the hopes
Of other souls that I have known.

And I wonder…

As I kneel in tears
With calloused hands and bleeding fingers
To sort through the pieces
Turning the fragments over
Piece by piece
Looking for something I cannot find

How did this happen?
How is it that I could not see
The turmoil as it came to pass?

01/05

Dreams 2

Have you ever looked into your heart,
And seen the wreckage of your wars?
Have you ever wondered…
How did this happen?

Have you ever had the courage,
To start again?
To assemble the pieces
Once more
And love as though there were no past
And there were no future?

That all there is,
Is the need to love for love's sake
And not any reward
For having done the right thing.

The error of our reason is often thus - -

We want the pay off
The adoration of our fellow travelers

But this is not what we are called to do - -

On this wheel of life.

01/05

Graham

Running through the grass,
Catching fireflies,
In the evening breeze.

And letting them go
And laughing
And saying how kind
And loving they are.

This is my son

Who teaches his dad
Without even trying
About living in the moment.

It really is that simple…

If we let it be so.

04/05

Isolation

They think they know the truth
But they only see the words
They think they know me
But have not my eyes

Without my feet
They cannot walk my road
Without my heart
They cannot feel my grief
Without my mind
They cannot see my vision

For I am a solitary man
And my journey is my own

And when I am done
It all shall end
The farce of life
The joy of life
The fear of life
The ignorance of life

It all shall end
And still,
In their silence
They shall….

        Not know why.

03/05

Laughter

He orbits life,
On the fringes of society.
He sees with different eyes,
Understanding not,
The ways of man.

His words fall in silence,
And create no echo in the heart.
His actions create currents,
Like an undertow,
Beneath the surface of the obvious.

Searching for an intersection point,
He tarries too long,
And stumbles,
In confusion.

Neither being a man,
Nor yet --
Becoming one
With all that is.

And in a moment of insight,
He laughs at himself,
And the arrogance of his ego…

And the lie it just told him.

07/05

Long, hard night

I.

In a paradoxical schism of self
I am not alone
And yet I am.

There is always with me…
The little boy
Inside

He stands in the corner of my life
Silent,
Waiting.

Too late to speak.

II.

There is no hope for me
In this cold, dark night
My life is a lost cause
An empty shell,
A shattered dream of inconsequence.

I cry for morning
But I wonder if it will ever come.

This night has a stony, unforgiving quality
It does not pardon
Or give release
And does not end.

III.

So here I sit
On the edge of the abyss
Unforgiven, unwanted.
By self or any other.

Too much the coward to live
Too much the coward to die

Is this how God feels?
Is this the other side of the hand?

IV.

I write each word with methodical slowness
As though somehow, time might go by faster
And dawn might arrive and give me hope.

But hope is only inside
Never out
Only what we choose to see or feel
In this momentary eternity
We call living.

And so the words,
Waiting to be erased
When I am gone
Fall one by one
Into the abyss
Into which I must surely follow.

Either now…

      Or later.

06/05

Mountaintops

A fellow traveler and I
Were together in a different place.

He said that here was a place,
Of mountains without valleys;

And in a moment of near-blinding insight
I saw the truth of his wisdom.

We create our own valleys
As places to hide
Rather than face the fear
Of standing on mountaintops.

Embracing opportunity,
Is harder than recoiling in doubt.

It is easier to try and fail
And say: "I told you so",

Than to do, and to succeed
And realize that we create

Our own mountaintops….

    …..from which to view our world.

10/05

Nagging Doubts

I sometimes have these nagging doubts…
That all I see around me
Is merely fabrication
An illusion of grand proportions.

What evidence is there of reality?
What is real?
What is truth?
What would I see
(for want of a better term)
If I were not confined by
Space and time?

Here and there, now and then
Would have no meaning
Change would not occur
I think also
That self and other
Would have no meaning

But I lack the skill or the courage
Or both
To make the discovery

So I remain….

       ….an unenlightened fool

Drowning in….

       ….my own delusion.

03/05

Pain

Is it through pain,
That we find the gifts of grace?

Is it in sadness,
That we find the value of joy?

Is it in loneliness,
That we find the enduring bonds of connection?

Is it in the opposites of life,
That we find its truths?

Is it for these reasons,
That we have not the sight,
To see the next step ahead?

For if we did,
Would any of us
Have the courage to take it?

01/05

Smile

I awakened from a meditation
And the world was as it always was
But I was not

Or did I awaken from a meditation
And the world was new
And I was unchanged?

I saw, not with eyes
But with my spirit

That all that is

Are merely reflections
Of something else…

Clues along the way
To guide the self-revealing
Awareness…

Of knowing why
The enlightened smile.

12/05

Smooth Stone

Is this a pebble?
Where once was rock?

Washed by experience,
Smoothed by life,
Sorted by cares.

The stone journeys onward
And says not a word
Yet hides nothing
From those
Who can read its tale.

Hard, smooth,
Tolerant, enduring
Reliable, resilient
Polished, silent,
Yet gentle to the touch.

Something to slip in a pocket

              …..And take home with you.

Who cares where it has been?
Only what it now is.

Few can see the pebble.
Fewer still can see beyond it.

04/05

Stranger to Self

There are days
When I read my words;
As though it were not I,
Who could possibly have written them.

What manner of man was it,
Who drew these words?

These words, so poignant
So full of grief - -
They slice across my heart.
And like a surgeon's scars,
Give history to the landscape of my soul.

When I look back,
In years to come;
Will I see myself as I truly am?
Will I see the poet?
Will the world be a better place,
For my having lived?

For if it is not for this
Why is it that my lungs draw breath?
That my heart beats still?
And my soul still aches for home?

In this short span of life
I am still a stranger to myself.

01/05

Struggle

I have struggled all my life;
As though the struggle,
Is the definition of my being.

Tossed about
In the maelstrom
Of my own making.

Yet I can control the winds,
And when I choose to do so,
I can raise my mind…
And the struggle ends.

Once more the moon,
Becomes itself --
In the surface of the lake.

And in returning,
We find
The essential calm,
That lies untouched
At the heart of the storm.

Until we choose once more,
To lower the mind
And let loose the demons,
Of delusion.

05/05

Train Ride

Trapped within my cubicle
Face pressed against the glass
Sweaty hands on cold glass
The train hurtles along

A blur of countryside
Night, day, night again
Light, dark, light, dark
I control nothing
I don't even know
The landscapes I pass

It is not my country
I'm not even sure
That this
Is the correct train

I recall buying a ticket
I do not recall that
The destination was
In any doubt

Curious, that.

04/05

Unwanted Child

I thought I was a little boy,
Unwanted and unlovable.
But I was wrong.

I thought I was a young man,
Foolhardy, blind and impetuous.
But I was wrong.

I thought I was a husband and a father,
Unforgivable and incapable.
But I was wrong.

Nothing happens within this Universe
Without the hand of God.

But I could never see
Through the eyes of God
Or see God's love
In every breath of life
And every vibration of being.

And so I never saw the truth
For what it was,
But only what I thought it ought to be.

06/05

Unwanted Offering

So he offered up his life
And it slammed into the wall of reason
Slithered down the sleek surface
And soaked into the carpet of past wrongs.

No one stooped to clear up the pieces
So they lay there…
Exactly where they fell
A pathetic pile of forgotten dreams
In a pool of blood red tears.

As a warning they lay there.
A warning that would go unheeded
By untold generations

But I was not there to see them.

06/05

Waiting for Spring

I have often wondered - -
Why we cause ourselves to suffer.
Why it is that we choose,
To take the difficult path,
To learning.

Why it is,
That only through our pain,
Do we learn compassion.

In the misty overcast dankness
Of a winter's day
The air is still and heavy.

And not unlike my soul…

Waiting for the breath of Spring,
And the warmth of new life.

01/05

Beginning

Looking for a beginning,
Halfway through the journey,
Is never easy.

Undoing the pathways of the past,
And erasing footsteps of the unwise,
Is not a thing that can be done.

But there are lessons here,
To be garnered with those whose souls,
Can still find truth.

Wisdom exacts a solid price,
And comes only to those
Who know suffering.

So the road is always ahead
And never back
Always onward.

We go forward
With eyes that have seen,
Hands that have done,
And hearts that know regret.

Perhaps we seek redemption
Or absolution for our past wrongs,
In the latter part of the journey.

Perhaps we simply seek to accept ….
Or understand
The choices that we made.

Perhaps we need not a new beginning
But a renewal of hope,
For the middle road can make us thirst
And test resolve of both heart and sinew.

It is always easy to give up and walk away.
It is never easy to forge ahead
And chance to find the God within.

09/06

Darkness

I know the darkness in my soul,
I have seen the long shadows,
In the fading night.

I have heard the distant footsteps,
And felt the breath,
Of the unwanted, unbeckoned foe.

And in the cold, hollow night,
I have feared to turn around,
And see the other face of self.

I have stood alone,
And failed, time and time again,
And falling, I have stood again.

It is my private pact,
With self and with no other;
That I shall in time,
Understand and overcome,
And learn the lesson of the darker self.

10/06

Lesson of the Toys

They make no judgments,
Have no expectations.
Eternally patient,
Never asking 'why'
Accepting all things,
Without exception,
With total commitment,
They give all they have;
Only to be forgotten or discarded,
Or treasured and loved --
And worn out or broken;
Or put away to be remembered in later years;
Or unwanted, or outgrown,
Given to another little boy.

My son and his toys,
Make a universe of possibilities;

And once again,
My son teaches his dad
And anyone who'll watch…
The magic stuff of life
That we forgot…
               when we grew up.

03/06

Plum Tree

I miss the Plum Tree
In the garden by the lake,
In which my son has climbed.

It was a home to bees
In the fragrant Spring of the year,
All covered with blossom,
And speaking silently of hope.

I miss the tree
That I felled.

Its death was not of my making,
But it left a void in my heart,
Just as it left a void by the lake.

A void that my son cannot climb.

I was sad for the loss of the ant-ravaged plum.
It was a home to bees,
And to the laughter of my son.

09/06

Prayer

Have you ever thought
That life with all its action
Is simply a prayer?

Have you stopped awhile,
Amid the storm
And felt the silence of surrender?

Have you stooped
To rake through the wreckage
Of broken homes,
Lost chances
Missed opportunities
And wayward paths
To discover that these too
Are part of the prayer?

It is only through giving way
That we see the truth
And by letting go
We open ourselves to wisdom.

It is not an easy path
It is not a well-trod path
For delusions will pull us all aside
And mire us in the doubts of ignorance
So that Pilgrim-like, we fall so easily
Into the Slough of Despair
And Dante-like we must go through all

If we are to see with different eyes.

Have you ever wondered why life is thus?

08/06

Sometimes

Air goes in and out,
And sometimes I breathe.
Muscles move back and forth,
And sometimes I flow.

Sometimes there is a mirror,
Sometimes there is me.
Sometimes I see,
But mostly I am blind.

Sometimes I struggle,
And sometimes I soar.
Sometimes I'm elegant,
And sometimes I'm sore.

Sometimes I'm a martial *artist,*
And sometimes I am simply at war.

Sometimes add themselves together
And the journey becomes the lesson.

12/06

Vignettes

Have you ever thought
That life
Is little more than a series of vignettes,
That we can never replay?

We take a role and play awhile
Then change the cast and change the scene
And enter another stage
In what seems to be
An unrelated plot.

So, looking back in later years
(In yet another role)
At that which then remains
We see the half remembered impressions
Of the scenes we played.
Tinged with nostalgia, regret or
Touched by joy
And perhaps a hint of the comic or the poignant
Filled with light and love or
Etched by darkness and fear

But seemingly, never do we see the full plot
For what it is, or was…
The raison d'être
That stays forever shrouded in mystery

Until at last the final curtain falls
And in that moment we gasp….

Ah yes….
    I see it now.

03/06

Ashes

Ashes of guilt surround me,
Burnt remains of past desires.

I leave footprints in their dust.

It was a muse who showed me
That ash, is merely dust.
Dust of what was,
Not what is.

So he shakes his body
And stands once more;

And the past falls away.

And in the fertile soil of the ash,
Grows the spiritual lotus we all seek.

All that remains,
Is to see it for what it is,
And to let it be.

It is that simple.

And in a sublime moment of joy….

        Give thanks.

05/07

Chasm

There is a bridge
Over the chasm of self-doubt.

It knows not of reason,
Nor of determination,
Or the will to succeed,
Nor tenacity of purpose.

In truth, each of these is needed,
And must be acquired along the pilgrim's road.
But the toll is not of this sort.

There is only one currency
That the sentinel will accept.

For in every vision…
Are the keys to success,
And the weapons of self-destruction.

How we see them,
How we use them…
Therein lies the wisdom of choice

As you place your foot ahead,
And touch the void,
And set your weight

The answer comes forth.

For, there is no other pathway…
No other bridge.

There is no other place to go
Between vision and reality,
Between crossing the chasm…
And falling headlong into the torrent below.

So, when strength fails and hearts would shrink away…
Remember that you are not alone,
For others too, have passed this way.

And they change the universe,
By what they do,
As they cross the void.

I now know why the bridge-keeper smiles;
As the toll is paid.

05/07

Loss

I miss the sea
As though a part of me were lost

I miss the waves, the sounds
The cliffs, the gulls
The storms

I feel as though
A part of me is missing

I miss the wind and rain
The unrelenting truth
And the sense of being that they bring

I feel alone
Or turned aside
From some path ordained

I have lost my way.

05/07

Muse

Setting.

She knows not her power
As she touches life.

She sees those around her
But not, I think, herself

Wise beyond reason
Yet innocent of life

A collection of resonant paradoxes
An old soul in a young frame…

Her eyes cannot hide
The truth of her being.

There, for all to see
Yet somehow, most do not.

Hers too is the path of the pilgrim.

Action.

And she will make of her life
An offering

Pouring out her heart
With not a moment breathed in regret

An amazing soul
I dare not touch
For fear of causing harm

A gift indeed
From whom we all could learn

To see and listen
And feel the hand of God.

05/07

Photographs

All the photographs are the work of Chris Dewey, except the photograph alongside the poem "***Lesson of the Toys***", which was the work of his wife, Janet.

With the exception of the title page photograph and the photograph on this page, which were taken at the Birmingham Gardens, AL, and the photographs alongside "***Beth***", "***Clouds***", "***Loss***" and "***Smooth Stone***" the other photographs were all taken in Mississippi.

About the Author

Chris was born in England, and received his doctorate in geology while he lived in Newfoundland, Canada. He moved to Mississippi in 1984, where he holds a faculty position at Mississippi State University.

Chris is part scientist, part martial artist, Reiki master, philosopher, poet, amateur photographer and avid reader. He has a deep love for the universe, the environment and for life. It may sound trite, but it is the driving desire to understand life, the meaning of the universe and the nature of the world around him that has led Chris into the life of the geologist, the world of the martial artist, and the labyrinth of the poet.

As a martial artist, he holds multiple black belts in Judo, Ju Jitsu, Hapkido and Taekwondo. Chris has been training in the martial arts since 1968, which coincidentally was the same year that he decided that he was going to become a geologist and a university professor when he grew up. Later, he decided not to grow up.

As a writer, Chris is a featured columnist for Martial Arts Professional Magazine and produces a monthly newsletter entitled "**Pathways**". He has published a three volume set of books concerning martial arts coaching as well as the first book of poetry entitled "**Paradox of Being**".